How to Belong

Also by Anne Collins
The Language of Water
My Friends, This Landscape
The Season of Chance
Seasoned with Honey (a four-poet anthology)

Anne Collins

How to Belong

Poems 2008–2018

How to Belong: Poems 2008–2018
ISBN 978 1 76041 802 1
Copyright © text Anne Collins 2019
annecollins.com.au
Cover: Anne Collins and Pen Tayler

First published 2019 by
Ginninderra Press
PO Box 3461 Port Adelaide 5015 Australia
www.ginninderrapress.com.au

Contents

I — 7
How to Belong — 9
Kinship — 14
Sliced Bread — 17
After the ambulance — 18

II — 19
Summer Beat — 21
Accent and Rhythm: Hobart/Seville — 22
Heatwave — 25

III — 27
Knowing Too Much, Yet Not Enough — 29
Virtual Reality — 31
Borders — 34
Lament — 36
Greeting to you and peace in your heart — 42

IV — 45
Returning to Amsterdam — 47
Shopping Just Because — 48
Harbour Lights — 49

V — 51
Reaching for the Still Point — 53
A Sense of Relief — 55
Peace — 56
A Womb of Trees — 57
Speaking to the Sea — 58

VI — 61
Falling Into — 63
Regarding the Invisible — 64

Notes — 65
Acknowledgements — 66

I

How to Belong

After the exhibition *Snapshot Photography and Migrant Women: A Tasmanian Experience*

I

I am the official story
with a barely-mentioned subtext.
Pieces of my jig-saw self are scattered
across a fraught landscape:
mine, yours, theirs.
Lives driven by
politics, poverty, danger, death,
 – and, for a few, adventure –
across imagination's borders.

II

In my snapshot
a three-year-old girl in a tartan kilt
stands erect, hands on hips
against a backdrop of gum trees.
I am she
the white child
invited to populate
this *British land short of people.**

---

* From the 1950s pamphlet of the Office of the Australian High Commission.

III

How to make a home away from home?
How to be a newcomer,
an outsider
how to live your life
in a language not your own?
My mother's accent underlined
the difference
between being an Australian like my father
or not.
What to take,
what to re-place elsewhere?
Bone-handled knives
virginal in their wedding gift box.
The door knocker in the shape
of a bagpipe player.
A claw-foot brooch.
Things that remind us
of who we think we are
in an unknown land
beyond promises,
with its upsidedown seasons,
its blinding light
its untold story.

IV

My parents preferred to get on with things
and not ask 'why?'
Our first home was a converted garage
four rooms on the edge
of an untamed backyard
by the banks of a flooding creek.
In the late 1950s our neighbours
were from England, Scotland, Holland,
Poland, Malta.
Only two families were from Germany
and one man's wife was from Japan.
In the early 1960s
the Italians came to live next door.
They gave my father home-made wine,
argued noisily, cooked with garlic and
invited us to a family wedding.
There at the age of seven
I first tasted pasta –
amidst the ravioli undulations of their speech.

V

My memory room displays
thin blue aerograms from Uncle Jackie,
the comics of *Oor Wullie* and *The Broons*,
oatcakes bought at Christmas and Scotch eggs –
the only time my mother allowed this word
to be used as an adjective.
Four floral soup bowls,
the last of my parents' first crockery set.
The Pedigree pram with its big wheels
and the trunk that carried the linen.
In the laminex wardrobe hangs
my mother's chiffon-velvet wedding dress
and her sequined black ball gown –
from before I was born –
both dresses abandoned
to time's unintended consequences.

VI

Since those days of the tartan kilt,
I've learnt about the lies
we were taught as fact
how the first peoples
– stolen from and stolen –
have been pushed to the edge
of our privilege
in this brash, adolescent country
we call Australia.
To remember most of us are
immigrants of one sort or another
is still subversive.
Since those days of the tartan kilt
I've been trying
to learn where I'm from
and where I belong –
my jigsaw self
a bit over there, a bit here, a bit nowhere.

Kinship

I

A thin line of words, morning chat,
little gifts, the latest photos,
catch-up gossip around the table
set with manners and obedience.
On the veranda watching parrots flash crimson,
an adult sister frowns her list of complaints.
Her hurry-boss mother ahead of the housework,
juggles pride with disappointment,
it seems there's little time
for soft-word luxury.
Her brother's off with a pie and his board –
the surf's good – to escape a hangover,
bickering, fatherhood, bad-mood mornings,
the niggle of irritation sparking like an electric fault.
A cigarette, a deep breath, a walk in the breeze,
she opens up worry with quick questions.

II

Late and defiant
her brother arrives home in a taxi,
scowls whisky breath across the room.
Her mother cries into the dishes, a pain in her chest,
her father sits with the TV flicker
and a knot in his veins.
In her dreams she runs away from being his sister,
from this tight-fright night,
wonders how little brothers turn into violent men.
The answer is blurred and grey.
In the morning she sits beside herself,
cries circles onto the lake.
Her mother reads, hums, cooks their favourite tea,
her grandad-father plays buckets and spades,
his grandsons' squeals trumpet delight.

III

A drive in the country, smiles in the car,
the toddlers play-call each person's name.
At the café they're like different people,
even a little urbane, a family gracious at lunch.
They all watch her brother,
his clean and sober freckle face
reminds her of the kid she knew,
the man his wife loves.
A storm cools their shame.

IV

Kitchen-table flowers smile colour,
evening chat mops up family history,
teasing recognition, elsewhere happiness,
card games, a sense of love between the lines.
The sky cries circles onto the lake,
the circumference of tears widens,
they belong to each other,
as the grit of sand to the sea-salt air.

Sliced Bread

Her father didn't believe in sliced bread,
their sandwiches were traditional
wobbly-white and thick,
cut with a knife. At thirty-three
he was all hot air and emphatic,
then silent as he thought a father should be.

At her first communion party,
a ruffle of dainty veils curtained the table,
pink-pretty with cupcakes and
sprinklings of hundreds and thousands.
A boy turned up his nose,
as he fingered the familiar
cubes bulky with egg.
She looked away,
chose a triangle slim with cheese,
the fairy-tale princess
determined to rise above the stares.

'Remember when you were so strict
about sliced bread?' she might have asked later
as her father buttered
a Tip Top square.
Their wars had long deflated
his authority-balloon
now wrinkled in the corner of memory
while she eats her bread
handmade, seeded,
with the tang of recall
as crumbs fall onto her chest.

After the ambulance

blood tests, angioplasty and a bag of drugs
I have my answer.
I am the unlikely-looking heart patient in a ward
with ruddy-faced men in pyjamas, who look as shocked as me –
these are the facts.
I take one day at a time, hold it up to the light,
remember
how the valium skated the surface of my body super-alert
as the experts wired their way
from inside my thigh to my coronary artery
to insert a tiny stent of surgical steel.

I measure time in pulse beats,
lucky to know aches and pains,
the clear blue sky beckons me.
They know so much about the heart, wrote W.S. Merwin.
Now I know about my heart, its inheritance.
It pumps with the strain of ancestors
centuries before us.

They're thinning my sticky blood
– just as they thinned my father's –
he was never going to make old bones, his mother said.
He died at 72 only nine years older than I am now.
Our vulnerable hearts, my father and I,
despite the strength in our hill-climbing calves
and our firm grip on things.
My old self-image is lost to this new knowledge.

II

Summer Beat

Being and doing and being in the doing, pruning and shaping, sorting and sifting, dancing and stretching, the being and doing, the music, the art, all day, all night, the beat, the life, the beat, the sun, the summer – beat, beat – beat it loud, softly beat beat goes the heart, the heart of who we are – beat beat – our hearts beat the heat of summer, in the being and the doing and the – beat – in between, beating the drums, the drumming and strumming of the heart ever onwards in the being, in the doing.

Accent and Rhythm: Hobart/Seville

In Hobart gums shed bark
onto cracked, thirsty ground.
Sunburnt trunks peel like skin,
moist underneath, almost delicate.
Moths and black insect specks
litter the lino.
We hanker for a thunderstorm
to quench the yellow grass,
relieve itchy eyes, clear the air of dust.

*

En Sevilla terracotta dust covers your shoes. At the Real Alcázar
a downpour patterns the paths,
gouges miniature runnels
into the compacted ground.

The heat clings.
Lying in the rich dark
watching a gecko stop and pace, stop and pace across the ceiling,
your languid body begs for sleep.

In the cobbled courtyard potted palms
stretch up to ozone blue.
Beyond the wall high like a monastery,
the maze of curved streets is quiet,
no scooter horns to warn
pedestrians moving along
the hem of footpath.

Evenings are freshly dressed with people
in lime-green, orange, pink and red
their *paseo* a promenade, colours flirt.
Children dash about the plaza,
behind trees and benches tiled in blue.

Andalucian pride is foot-stamping, fierce, forthright,
con brio y gusto
old ladies muscle about in noisy groups.
Their conversation greets the twilight,
an offbeat full of promise.
Fireworks laughter cracks open the night.

*

At a beach in Hobart
our Celtic skins, pink and freckled, are too delicate.
The casual chat of lives
is scattered across the sand in fragments…'neurologist'
a man says in tones of defiance…'brain tumor.'
These are words I understand, yet I'm still left to imagine.
At the edge of this sea-river
parents dip their babies into waves,
dogs cavort, sprinters arrow past
girls in new bikinis call 'Roxy, Sheba'
to Christmas puppies wet and wobbly.

There's no frill in the voice, no wailing song,
it's the space here that's permissive,
fewer people make a crowd.
In the background a mountain darkens
over this tiny city, its heart a *pueblo*,
and the riot of a red sky
clear of smoke, still, no wind,
readies for a full moon.

Heatwave

Adelaide, March 2008

The house waits for the dawn easterly
to billow its curtains cool.
A single sheet feels too hot,
there's nothing to breathe,
after a sleepless night
my brain befuddles to zero,
my feet and hands swell tight.
Maroon, mineral-smelling blood
gushes wasted from my womb.

Thick and dry as sandpaper
heat burdens every move
one foot in front of the other
almost impossible. My arm reaches over,
to put a cup down on the bench, I stare blank
into the haze,
its molecules scratch my face.
The closed-up house swells tight.

In air-conditioned galleries I ponder art,
then sweat at the bus stop in a strip of shade.
A crisp, high-heeled wedding party, feathered and buffed
perfumes the footpath.
The crowded bus full of tolerant-looking faces
is slowed by traffic, it stops – jerks –
a woman struggles with her baby
but declines the offer of a seat.
The Bluetooth man from Sudan
shrugs and smiles his words into the gritty air.

At the writers' festival in the park voices
drift across the swelter to those
fanning metaphors in the shade.
Later, lost in the glare of an empty street
where squat stone houses frown at parched gardens
I calculate the direction to my friend's house
waiting dark and cool, fan swirling,
rehearse 'first right, second left'
but in reverse I'm stuck.

The heat leaves me heavy-lidded on the couch,
presses on my head as I read then surrender to cushions.
Conversation in the other room fades
as if someone pressed the volume button.
Dreams come rushing in.
Did I come all this way to sleep?

The evening temperature is exotic
under the restaurant's palms
with gin and tonic. Friends talk about death,
joke that intelligent people are nocturnal,
don't say 'it's hot'.
My shimmer-shirt clings pink,
my legs peel from retro-vinyl chairs.
In the lantern-lit night-park we mingle with the crowd
dust in our hair and throats
heat-drugged and travelling in music from around the world
in the breezeless air.

III

Knowing Too Much, Yet Not Enough

After the film *Human Flow* by Ai Weiwei

At the art-house cinema this film shows me
what I already know. I am here to not ignore, to not forget,

to pay attention to this record of human tragedy
spreading across the screen in a two-and-a-half hour story.

In emails other crises also demand my attention
but today I delete them. My privilege is that

I can't always give it. Once upon a time
a sticker on my fridge said *maintain your outrage* –

many of us still write letters, stand with placards on street corners,
knit our resistance into quilts, raise funds, sign petitions, deliver them

to people living behind the walls of power and politics.
Three people in the cinema, this is not a blockbuster, should it be?

A blockbuster number of people – sixty-five million – are
fleeing for their safety in real time – not virtual, not reality TV,

not a thriller – moving on and on beyond the screen. History
happening frame by frame. I am writing in the dark. A white bird glides

above a stretch of blue sea where a boat drifts with people
wearing orange life vests like the ones abandoned on the shores of Europe

and captured by a drone camera as if the scene were an abstract painting.
In the trudging from place to place, the quiet lack of media spin

has to count for something. In another frame a family returns to their shell
of home, picks through the wreckage of streets and apartments, blackened,

twisted, gaping. The camera catches a corner of colour, a remnant of floral
couch shiny like silk, exposed like entrails. How like us these people

really were in their once-comfortable lives. This is their story. My story
is this: after the film I walk home, try to imagine my middle-class suburb

turned inside-out by war. The green peace of my garden feels somewhat surreal,
as does the gentle rain on the veranda roof. Why is showing compassion so brave,

so feared, so despised? Why have four small words 'we can do it' cost the career
of a politician who grew up behind a wall? What now? Attend the next rally,

write again to the government, ring them? Donate time, money,
campaign for kindness? Question how I travel? Ask why again and again?

Virtual Reality

I

This holiday village
with a neatly organised beach
protects the hooded plovers
and the well-graded walking paths through
the she-oaks and gums along the cliff top.
A faded sign pinned to a tree
warns of snakes but they moved away
long ago to safer ground.
Council signs stand like sentinels
where once there were trees,
threatening fines for any further removal.

Below the clifftop
a steep quarry
where sandstone was cut in straight lines
to build cities for the colony.
Nearby, vacant villas crowd the view
waiting – as if they've been put to sleep –
for their people
to get away from real life
and come back here.

On the beach
an oystercatcher's beak
startles red in the sunset.
Nothing, it seems,
could be more real than this.
The cliffs crumble grain by grain,
if left alone they will outlive us all.

Evening birds flutter and dart
from branch to bush
their language a chittering,
tuttering, wip-wip wipping.
And then a sudden oik! from the bigger wattlebird,
as if to say hey, move over!
On Friday night the holiday village lights up
beneath the glow of a half-moon.
People have come to rest and play.

II

What could be more real
and less absurd than this?
Certainly not the news of the world
littered with body parts.
So too the sand is littered
with left-over crab-bits from a gull's dinner.
The sea's an aqua-green, clear as glass.
The ocean is telling us to quieten down.
*So much depends…*the great poet said.
So much depends
on the light and the cast
of lines and shadows,
how much you can see,
how much you want to see.

III

Is this less real
than the news I read
about bombs in Beirut or Paris,
shootings in Sydney;
or the terrorist who asked his wife
to send him shampoo, deodorant
to the distant battlefield?
The suicide-bomber was a party girl with a reputation
and an abusive past –
so the story goes –
drugs and sex, addicted
to screens and selfies.
Blowing herself to pieces,
was how she got away.

IV

I go for a walk, get some air
but there's something wrong.
When the light's too bright
the sun feels like it could burn
through layers of history and angst to bone.

This land's not ours.

V

And the waves
and the birds –
who belongs to them?

Borders

You travel uncertain paths
cross fate's borders on foot
or in unsafe trucks and boats.
Your despair
unravels on our shores.
Authorities spin-dry the details
– call you illegal –
as if you'd left behind the good life.
I watch
our national compassion drown
in the swell of lies.

The Frequent Flyer ad invites me to *Get away sooner*.
My travel relies on safety rules and insurance.
On a plane
a man sitting amongst business people and holiday makers
is being deported back to torture.
The flip side of customer service is to lock you up,
tag you by number, ask questions later.

In my quietest moments I know
*there by the grace of god…*does it matter whose god?
The ambitions of those schooled in the cruelties of success
fail history and poetry:
once we had a country and we thought it fair.*

You live on the edge of our awareness.
You sew your lips together because you feel betrayed
and we are shocked or worse, cynical.
Later it's your courage and your generosity
that confront us the most
– when, after all that, you can say:
I believe in the Australian law
I trust the Australian people.

You do not trespass.
Your dignity confronts our shame.
In punishing you, we punish ourselves.

* From 'Refugee Blues' by W.H. Auden.

Lament

A Suite of Six Poems

I

Mei Ling was born crying
in a rubbish pile.
She sells roses to 'go away' tourists
for a bowl of noodles at night,
sits in a huddle of little girls
in floral Mandarin jackets, grubby
and waiting for the boss to come.
They stare out beyond danger
and the ghost of pain,
their eyes stunned round like dolls.

Mei Ling stands at a school gate,
watching the laughter in the playground,
imagines who she might have been.

II

Zico and Lara pull carts
heavy with cans and cardboard
on streets jammed with BMWs
and gleaming blue glass.

The rich move by helicopter
from one skyscraper to another,
avoiding the thin, tired children
like Zico and Lara asleep on the bus.
Beneath the blue
in their scrap hamlet
they count their reais,
remember
the sweet taste of half an orange,
and the promise
of another recycled tomorrow.

III

A group of boys in rags
clutching assault rifles, moves
through fields of lush green maize.
The sun heats their fears,
they wait, watch, then shoot
other boys coming towards them
in crisp khaki camouflage.

Ekene surveys the enemy's village,
from a hill top,
neat mud-huts and skipping girls below.
He follows orders,
breaks padlocks at night,
steals into classrooms with bombs,
reads tomorrow's questions on the board,
writes chalk answers, pleased
he knows the capital of France is Paris.

Sitting at a desk,
Ekene falls asleep in tears,
dreams
of a time before he was kidnapped.

IV

Unity hides her bad blood medicine
and comforts her parents
who shoot-up in the bathroom.

At the park she rides
the swings of rage and fear.
Spoiling for a fight,
other girls schooled in prejudice
throw her sandwich on the ground
ram her head into the fence,
yell 'your skin's too white',
bark at her heels like a pack of dogs.

One day Unity walks tall
hand-in-hand with her parents
through the streets that breed rumours,
to the teenage health clinic
determined to talk about AIDS.

V

At a bus station children
play the *zurla*, smoke cigarettes, gypsy-gyrate,
charm the waiting, ticket-selling people
to dance and drift on the lift of melody
and party away their boredom.

In a few cute moves nimble fingers pick pockets,
stuff cash beneath shirts,
deposit the day's takings
into their father's vodka-sipping hands.
He kisses them all with pride –
except for Blasko who refused
to steal. Just out of prison
he is stunned
by the blow to his head from his father's fist.

Blasko hurls himself back
behind those high grey walls.
There he is
the barber, the goalkeeper, the bedtime storyteller
and the singing is regulated
by a steady beat
that permits a nine-year-old boy
to stop being a thief.

VI

Luca plays shadow puppets,
animal silhouettes sharpened
by Neapolitan light and a mother's shouts
about the cost of her accidental son.

Luca toughs it out,
rips a Rolex from a cufflinked arm,
runs fast enough.
At the piazza a dealer buys the watch,
Luca buys fairy floss
and heads for the carnival.

His almond eyes fringed in ebony
want
the moving circle of rainbow ponies,
its gentle, beautiful, baby stuff.

Greeting to you and peace in your heart

Hello, Ghulam,
I am writing to tell you there are people in Australia who care,
we do not agree with our government's policies.

> *Dear friend, greeting to you and peace in your heart.*
> *Before I left my country I was in prison for three years,*
> *I have not lived free from age 15.*

I live in Tasmania. Most people I know
want better treatment for refugees,
I am sending you the English books you asked for.

> *I am deprived of everything except sorrow and razor-wire.*
> *I was born with grief,*
> *my future seems dark and invisible.*

Dear Ghulam, do not give up hope, you are more than a number.
People here are working to make things better,
you are doing very well with your English.

> *I apologise for delay in replying to your letter.*
> *As you are aware, some of us were*
> *in hunger strike for a month.*

I was very sad to hear your news.
I hope things get better for you soon,
you are not forgotten, you are more than a number.

> *Dear friend, what is the real meaning of freedom and democracy?*
> *I want to understand it, I did not experience it,*
> *I don't know what it is yet.*

Dear Ghulam, democracy is complicated.
We vote but sometimes people we don't like win power,
most of us in Australia can criticise our governments.

> *This is my photo taken at Nauru Detention Centre,*
> *I am with the children who are in detention,*
> *please don't give my photo on the internet.*

In Australia we have freedom and we have laws:
if we obey the laws most of us can do
what we want in life. But freedom can be unjust.

> *Dear friend, I become sick like depression, I use tablet.*
> *I can't sleep at night,*
> *has man learned how live like human being?*

Dear Ghulam, when we have freedom, or think we do,
we hardly notice it
until it is taken away.

> *Dear friend, I couldn't believe one day I would get free*
> *from Nauru hell. We got free from prison*
> *after suffering and punishment.*

I am so pleased a country has welcomed you.
I am sorry you have suffered
because of Australian politics.

> *We took off from Nauru airport.*
> *I was brimful of crying excitement,*
> *I was flying over clouds and the beautiful ocean.*

I am happy you are starting a new life.
I wish you all the best,
I hope everything goes well for you.

> *Dear friend, I am joyful to be in New Zealand paradise.*
> *I have nothing at the moment*
> *but I am very optimistic about my future.*

Dear Ghulam, I hope you are still optimistic. My heart is heavy: 17 years after the Tampa, our governments are even more cruel, our letters are now *returned to sender* in boxes from Manus Island and Nauru.

IV

Returning to Amsterdam

Perhaps it's too much stirring of memory, perhaps
there's no refuge in fiction after all.
Looking back three decades, we rallied in millions
against the doom of the nuclear age,
though we never predicted the apocalypse of viral money.
'Amsterdam is a farce.'
my Dutch friend said, as if she meant a theme park.
We walk up and down the canals,
remember how it was in our youth and search like two
homeless philosophers
through the litter of tourist clichés for some kind of meaning.
Alain de Botton's claim
that ART IS THERAPY displayed in neon on the wall
of the newly renovated Rijksmuseum
is hardly a consolation. At the Anne Frank Huis people wait
in long queues to get close
to its story, for me the daily news is enough.
It's the Resistance Museum that reminds us
of fascism's administrative efficiency. Fiction is what we crave
– once upon a time I was the one here cleaning hotel rooms,
busking at the Centraal Station and laughing my way through a year
I haven't laughed like that since.
Now, long after the wall collapsed
Russian maids my own ripe age service us with fresh towels.
Do they feel lucky to have their jobs
cleaning the crimson and pink luxury of this family hotel?
How much do they get paid?
We come and go with our baggage full of assumptions
and our claims to a past
no one under 50 is interested in.

Shopping Just Because

The woman in the too-tight business suit
standing at the traffic lights
has just done the sales.
A rumble of log trucks, delivery vans, four-wheel drives
gusts past, grits her eyes behind sleek black frames.
She frowns,
clutches her jumbo plastic bags
against the pressure
of wanting to be somewhere else, someone else
without the need for all these things
keeping her kerbed,
her lunch hours on a leash,
pulling her into a future so hectic
where desire is push-buttoned, remote-controlled, flat-screened
and the past is an endless pile
of discarded, disposable, unfixable things,
yesterday's promise of a better life, guaranteed not to last.

Harbour Lights

The city's importance dissolves
in a swirl of colour. The up and down week
is over. Casting aside my old routines,
the patterns that have shaped me,
old-home harmonies,
I stand on the edge of a year,
look into the liquid light, imagine
swimming in it, coming up all energetic yellow.
Walking along the pier of curiosity
I glow red in a new landscape.

V

Reaching for the Still Point

Five contemplations

I could hear the humidity in her voice
the build-up of sentences.
Our minds ached.
We stretched our thoughts around
the possibility of words, then craved silence.

*

All my papers are neatly stacked,
the novel, the essays, the poetry
ready for their moment. Perhaps
there's room for philosophy. As poets
we pay serious attention to rhythm, syllables, images, colour,
to stories told in stanzas, to commas, full-stops,
to the shade of pigment, tone, light and line.
Is this when we count our achievements?

*

When noise threads every experience from hum to roar,
it traps the city
on the move with planes, traffic, trains, machines
and a trendy mood – ironic, pushing ahead
to the next thing, the next place
where money is the fiction that buys things.
Babies howl beneath the monster scream of jets overhead
minute by minute. The cardboard box man
sits in the tunnel, patiently asks for change.

At the homelessness rally people defy authority,
feel the pain of it. On the edge of tiredness
daydreams linger. Any peace found in these urban cracks
is a blessing. The comfort zone is crepe myrtle footpaths,
keep-out calm: no eye contact, bars on windows and doors,
lest you lose yourself looking for a smile.

*

In the cool, clean morning back on the island
a tawny frogmouth marks a slow, persistent 'oom'.
A spider jumps from the ceiling, its legs splayed.
Near the lake the silence has no background buzz,
it's thicker, heavier, waits in welcome
beneath the trees curtained by half-moon mist.

*

In the privilege of space, solitude, conversation, listening,
there are gardens to tend, languages to learn,
mathematics to teach, the oxygen of dance
to keep your brain and back strong
and the shadow of night-worry receding.

A Sense of Relief

It's a relief to turn the lights out
to lie down in the dark
to wrap a wall of wave-sound around my silence
to open the doors and let my thoughts out
it's a relief to watch the sun go behind the hills
to know the first evening stars are a glimpse of the past
it's a relief to follow this Buddhist instruction:
don't just do something, sit there
to notice the ticking clock, its arbitrary measure of time
to know that time can't be saved
it's a relief to close my eyes
to be here now.

Peace

Peace is a quiet winter morning. Peace is the taste of freshly brewed tea on your tongue knowing the tea workers have been fairly paid. Peace is gratitude for your fortunate life and the comfort of a warm house facing a green hillside where some of the trees have been saved. Peace is speaking kindly to your loved ones, your neighbour, your friends, acquaintances, to yourself, the people you meet in shops, on the street, on the bus. Peace is making a garden and feeling blessed by it. Peace is noticing your breath. Peace is walking in the bush after rain, feeling safe in the company of currawongs and the smell of damp eucalypt. Peace is a mind not crammed with thoughts, a mind with spaces, a mind that doesn't have to hurry. Peace is a day free of emails. Peace is letting go the need to berate others. Peace is cooperation, compassion, empathy. Peace is not mute. Peace tells the truths about war and injustice. Peace is a way of seeing. We hope for it, we work at it. Peace is beyond religion and philosophy. Peace takes its time. Peace celebrates those remarkable goodwill stories that rarely make the news, stories of people breaching the boundaries that divide us.

A Womb of Trees

'…there are realms where souls
crushed by the weight of the world
find refuge.'*

When you want to go back
tunnel into the trees, feel your body
soften, your mind clear, no need
to think, the caress of shadow, the cool relief,
curl back into the animal you once were
and before that, a speck of possibility
in the air, relive your pre-birth potential
when you drifted in a rich dark universe.
Listen to the whisper of the she-oaks, know
their poise, their fine needle-like foliage perfectly
segmented. Feel eternity, here, now. Delay
your departure towards the light
that shimmers blue, a vast ocean where
waters will break again and a cry will be heard
before the next rush of reality.

* From the poem by Rosalia de Castro titled 'From the Cadenced
  Roar of the Waves'.

Speaking to the Sea

If I lived here would I start to ignore you
or would you become a part of me
as familiar and unnoticed as my pulse?
It's hard to imagine
that I would not pause each day,
and put my busyness on hold,
just to adore you.
Even when you have a temper
I enjoy watching you
from inside this house perched on rocks.

Hush you say, hush, hush. At night
you stir my imagination
and play with my dreams. In your presence
a new morning lights up like a promise
and for a few moments
the hard world, with all its bad news,
seems like a nightmare
that perhaps we humans could wake-up from
and on waking, remember
to respect life.

When I die
I want to become a rock by the sea
where I can be weathered pebble smooth
or abstract jagged by the waves of time
still to come,
outlasting the history of human folly.
Then I would be
forever in your ebb and flow
holding steadfast – even in your turmoil –
until the earth surrenders to the sun
and once again we all become
stardust.

VI

Falling Into

A meditation on creative practice

Falling into the half-sleep of a poem
nudging the light of day
that zone of rapid-eye dreams
> – suddenly in the thick blue middle
> of action, like tuning into a movie midway
> falling into some strange yet familiar plot
> a sequence of events, the pressing details
> of getting this or that done, going this way
> or that with people central to the story
> yet you hardly know them –

then half-waking again as the morning light lengthens
and the room comes into focus for a minute or two
> – then falling back into that heavy-lidded
> inner, outer-space
> where there is no falling, no up or down
> just a drifting, timeless passing
> a weightless movement, an enfolding
> of slate-grey and a spot of yellow,
> you might say a sun right of centre
> but there is no centre
> there is no right or left, no wrong
> falling into and away from
> the need for prepositions and adverbs –

the galaxy of the imagination, alive to
the tilt, the lift, the pleasure.*

---

* Reference to *Turning* by Denise Levertov.

Regarding the Invisible

Loops of light dance from rock to rock, magnetic lines
traced from the smell of stone.
Does the earth push up against the weight bearing down on it?
Einstein's gravity equals acceleration.
What am I?
I remember
leaping from boulder to boulder
a charge travelling through my bare feet
as they kissed the dolerite.

Any notion of being still
rotates into the future at 1,241 kilometres per hour*
beyond day and night.
Some cultures know rock as family.
Science says the past is out there
in its own space-time
sending us light.
I am nothing
if not grounded in stone.

---

* The speed of the earth's rotation at latitude 42 degrees.

Notes

'How to Belong' after the exhibition *Snapshot Photography and Migrant Women: A Tasmanian Experience*, Tasmanian Museum and Art Gallery, 2016.

'Lament' after the film *All the Invisible Children*, an anthology of short films curated by Chiara Tilesi and Stefano Veneruso, 2005.

'Harbour Lights' after the painting *Symphony of Harbour Lights* by Chen Ping.

'A Womb of Trees' after the exhibition *The Long Game* by David Keeling, Dick Bett Gallery, 2016. Paintings about Narawntapu National Park, Tasmania.

Epigraph from the poem by Rosalia de Castro titled: 'From the Cadenced Roar of the Waves' in *Rosalia de Castro Selected Poems* https://theinkbrain.wordpress.com.

'Falling Into' after the painting *Falling Into* by Chen Ping.

'Regarding the Invisible' after *Field Lines*, an exhibition by Cameron Robbins, MONA, 2016.

Acknowledgements

Many poems in this collection were first published (some as earlier versions) in the following journals, anthologies and projects:

Famous Reporter, 2008
Endangered (an exhibition), Hobart, 2008
A Net of Hands, FAW Tasmania, 2009
Another Lost Shark, poetry blog, 2009
Blue Dog Journal, 2009
First Refuge, Ginninderra Press, 2016
Writing to the Wire, UWA Press, 2016
Prospect, 2010, 2016
Tamba, 2015, 2017
Communion, 2017
Social Alternatives, 2017, 2018
Stories in September (narrated poem), State Cinema, Hobart, September 2018.

Many thanks to fellow poet Anne Kellas for her insightful feedback on an earlier draft of this collection. Many thanks to Kath McLean for also responding to this earlier draft and for her excellent proofreading, as well as for her ongoing support of my writing life over many years. Sincere thanks to Pen Tayler for her technical skills, generosity and patience in assisting with the cover design.

www.ingramcontent.com/pod-product-compliance
Lightning Source LLC
Chambersburg PA
CBHW072208100526
44589CB00015B/2436